My Sister Kim

Contents

My Sister Kim

Marian Iseard

Published in association with
The Basic Skills Agency

Hodd

A MEMBER O

Acknowledgements
Cover: Stephanie Hawken
Illustrations: Jim Eldridge

Orders; please contact Bookpoint Ltd, 39 Milton Park, Abingdon, Oxon OX14
4TD. Telephone: (44) 01235 400414, Fax: (44) 01235 400454. Lines are open
from 9.00–6.00, Monday to Saturday, with a 24 hour message answering service.
Email address: orders@bookpoint.co.uk

British Library Cataloguing in Publication Data
A catalogue record for this title is available from the British Library

ISBN 0 340 77613 7

First published 2000
Impression number 10 9 8 7 6 5 4 3 2 1
Year   2005 2004 2003 2002 2001 2000

Typeset by GreenGate Publishing Services, Tonbridge, Kent.
Printed in Great Britain for Hodder and Stoughton Educational, a division of
Hodder Headline Plc, 338 Euston Road, London NW1 3BH, by Atheneum
Press, Gateshead, Tyne & Wear

1

Kim

What can I tell you about my sister?
That she's clever?
That she's kind?
That she's funny and great fun to be with?
Yes, she's all those things. Everyone says so.

So why is it that I worry about her?
Well there is another side to Kim.
She doesn't like being told what to do.
Never has. And it gets her into trouble
– at home and at school.

Kim is fifteen, and I'm two years older.
If I had a pound for every time
someone has said to me,
'Your sister Kim, she's in trouble again!'
I'd be very rich.

I mean, don't think that I'm
a little goody-goody because I'm not.
It's not that I never do anything wrong,
but Kim – she seems to *look* for trouble.

Like when she bunks off school,
or when she's rude to the teachers.
Like when she screams at Mum
that she can't rule her life
and slams out the door.
Or stays out until half-past eleven
when she should have been back at ten.
Or tells them she's with me when she isn't.

Most of the time I try not to get involved,
but sometimes I just have to have a go at her.
Then she gets mad with me and we argue.

I tell her she's childish
and she tells me I'm boring and no fun.
I guess we'll never see eye-to-eye.

Still, I never thought Kim
would do anything really bad.
It was always stuff to kick against
the grown-ups.
As if she was saying,
'You can't tell me what to do'.
Dad said it ran in the family.
His brother had been just the same.
'She'll grow out of it,' he'd say,
'like Stuart did.'

I don't know when exactly I began to get
really worried. I suppose it was soon after
she got friendly with Kelly and Dawn.
She'd never really bothered with them before.
All of a sudden they were a threesome.
I used to see them together after school,
when I was on my way home from college.
They were always hanging around the shops.

Buying make-up and stuff.
Every day Kim seemed to have
some new lipstick, or a different eye-shadow.

'You must spend all your money on make-up,'
I said to her one day.

She just shrugged. 'It's not a crime, is it?'

For some reason, that comment
stuck in my mind.

2

New Clothes

One Saturday Kim went into town
with Kelly and Dawn.
I knew for a fact she had no money.
I'd had to lend her some the day before.
She came home with a new top.
Mum was there.
We were just making a cup of tea.
She looked up.
'That's nice Kim,' she said.
'I thought you were broke!' I exclaimed.
'How come I had to lend you some
money yesterday?'

'Oh this is out of my birthday money,'
she said. 'I didn't spend it all.
Here you are.'
She tossed a pound coin onto the table.
'Birthday money? Your birthday was
months ago!'
'Well I saved some, didn't I?'

She snatched her new top off the table
and went upstairs in a huff.
Mum told me to stop going on at her.
She said it was good that Kim
had saved some birthday money
and not spent it all at once.
I didn't say anything,
but it just didn't feel right.
Kim never saves anything.
I was worried that Kelly and Dawn
were lending her money.
Kim might be getting into debt.
Spending money that she didn't have.
How would she ever pay it back?

Sometimes Kim would wear clothes
I hadn't seen before.
'Where did you get that?' I would ask.
'Swapped it with Dawn,' she'd say.
Or, 'Kelly said I could have it,
she doesn't like it anymore.'
But the clothes always looked brand new.

One day I did something
I have never done before.
Well, only when I was little and I thought
Kim had hidden one of my toys.
I waited until she was out,
then I went into her bedroom.
I started looking through her wardrobe.
It wasn't long before I found
what I was looking for.
At the back, well hidden,
was a little heap of clothes.
New clothes. Some still had the price tag on.
Now I knew what was going on.

Kelly and Dawn couldn't possibly
lend her money for all these.
Kim must have stolen them.
She was shoplifting.
I went hot and cold, both together.
Could Kim really be stealing clothes?
I looked at the labels on the clothes.
Some were from posh shops
and would have cost a fortune.

It was then that I knew I was right.
What was I going to do about it?

I couldn't tell Mum and Dad,
that was for sure.
They had enough to worry about
ever since Dad had been made redundant.
Mum was working lots of extra hours
at a supermarket.
Dad spent his days filling in forms
or down the job centre.
In the evenings he worked as a security guard.
I suppose that's why it had been only me
who'd noticed Kim and her clothes.
They were just too busy.

I thought about talking to Ian.
That's my boyfriend. But I was too proud.
I didn't want him to think Kim was a thief.
It was down to me to do something.
I had to get Kim to stop what she was doing.
I knew I had to talk to her
before she got into serious trouble.

3

I-Spy

The next Saturday I overheard Kim
talking to Dawn on the phone.
She was going to meet Kelly and Dawn
in the town.

'Outside Boots, two o'clock,'
she said to Dawn. 'See you there.'
I went all prickly.
It was then that I decided to follow her.

I went out before her and sat
in the coffee shop across the road from Boots.

It wasn't long before I saw her
meet up with the others.
I watched them. They were heading for Taylors
– a big department store.

I followed them across the square.
Once Kim turned round to look at something.
I stopped and pretended to do up my shoe.
When I looked up I couldn't see them!
I rushed into the shop.
There they were, at the perfume counter.
As I watched I saw Kim
slip something into her bag –
now there was no doubt.
Next they went up the escalator.
I guessed they were going
to the clothes department.
I waited a minute. Then I went up the stairs
on the other side of the shop.
I could see them but they weren't
looking my way. They were too busy.

I watched Kim pick up a blue shirt.
She went towards the changing rooms.
She walked behind a rack of clothes.
When I next saw her the shirt had disappeared
– and she hadn't put it back
where it came from.

That was when I spotted the woman.
She was watching Kim.
She had a two-way radio in her hand
and she was speaking into it.
My heart sank. Kim was about to get caught.
I had to do something. Fast.
Without thinking what I was going to say
I went over to Kim.
When she saw me her face went bright red.
She looked really angry.
'What are you doing here Sophie?' she said.

I tried to get Kim to come with me.
'Kim – you're being watched.
The store detective has seen you.
Just put everything back and come with me.'
Kelly and Dawn heard me.
They disappeared pretty quickly.
'Put what back?' Kim said.
'What are you talking about?'

'Kim, I know what you've been doing.
Put the things back and leave.'
'You're mad. I don't know what you mean.
Just leave me alone!'

I couldn't believe it. She was about to get done
and here she was arguing with me.
And all the time the evidence
was right there in her bag ...

4

Caught in the Act

Suddenly Kim stormed off. I ran after her.
Down the escalator, banging into people.
'Sorry!' I shouted to one woman.
Now Kim was running. So was I –
along with the woman with the radio.
People were looking.
As Kim ran out of the shop
a man caught hold of her.
'OK, stop there, both of you.'

The woman held my arm.
The man had hold of Kim.
The woman must have called him on the radio.
'We have reason to believe you have taken
things from this store without paying.
I'd like you to come up to
the manager's office please. This way.'

I knew it was useless to do anything else.
I felt so ashamed.
I just hoped no one who knew me was watching.
On the way upstairs
I thought about what to do.
I thought I could explain my part in this,
and try to get them to let Kim go.
I would say she'd never done it before.
Or that she wasn't well.
Or maybe that her boyfriend
had just dumped her – anything.
I was prepared to lie, for Kim's sake.
As long as she kept quiet.

For once she did. She seemed to be in shock.
I suppose up to now it must have seemed like
a big game to her – but this was no game.

The manager looked like my old maths teacher.
He had a face that looked like it had heard
all the excuses before.

'Empty your bags please,' he said.
I took everything out of my handbag.
Kim emptied her big canvas bag.
Out came the bottle of perfume
and the blue shirt.
'Do you have receipts for these?' he asked.
She shook her head.
'Then I'm afraid I shall have to
call the police.'

Kim's face had gone white.
She didn't say anything.
I didn't know what to say either.

The manager looked at me.
'You, I suppose, were the lookout?'
'She's my sister,' said Kim.
'She's got nothing to do with it.
She was trying to stop me.'

Suddenly I found my voice.
'She's never done this before. She's upset –
her boyfriend has just finished with her.
She'll never do it again.'
Kim looked at me, mouth wide open.
Just don't say anything, I willed her.
Let me do the talking.

The manager looked at me.
Then he looked at Kim.
'I'm sorry,' he said.
'We always call the police.
If we let you off – why not all of them?'

He picked up the phone
and tapped out a number.
There was nothing to do now but wait.

5

The Lie

The police arrived.
There were two of them, a man and a woman.
The store detective told them what she'd seen.
She told them what we'd said.
Then the policewoman told us
we were going to be taken down to the station.

It was all becoming like a bad dream.
Walking through the store
with the police at our side.

Getting into a police car
at the back of the shop.
Driving through town,
hoping that no one would see us.
Then into the station.

They put us in a cell.
'It's just until your parents get here,'
the policewoman said.
She was trying to be kind.
She could see what a shock it was to us.

When we were alone Kim began to cry.
I put my arm around her.
'Why were you there?' she asked.
'I just happened to see you.
I'd gone to buy a pair of jeans,' I lied.
'I've never done this before,' she said.
I didn't say anything.
I didn't tell her what I knew.
I thought it was best if she didn't know –
for the time being at any rate.

Mum and Dad came.
They were both upset
but we didn't have a chance to talk.
First they went into the interview room
with Kim. Then with me.
I told the police what I'd told Kim.
That I just happened to be shopping
and saw her take the shirt.
After all, what was the point
of saying anything else?
It would only make things worse.

Afterwards they brought Mum and Dad
a cup of tea. We sat and waited.
No one spoke much.
We seemed to wait for an age in that room.
Finally the policewoman came back.
She said that because it was her first offence
Kim would be let off with a warning.

'Well Kim,' she said, shutting her notebook.
'I hope you've learnt something today.
It may seem clever, to go stealing.
But it's not so clever
when you get caught, is it?'

Mum and Dad took us home.
They couldn't believe what had happened.
Mum kept asking Kim why she'd done it.
She asked if she was unhappy at home
– as if it was *her* fault.

They quizzed me too.
I stuck to the lie I'd made up.
I didn't see what else I could do.
My biggest fear was that they would do
what I'd done – go and look in Kim's wardrobe.
Luckily they didn't seem to think of that.

Kim was grounded for a week.
Mum took some time off work,
so she could be home in the evenings.
She looked tired, and suddenly older.

I think that was when
I started to feel angry with Kim.
So angry I couldn't even speak to her.
She wasn't talking to me anyway.
Not even to say thanks for lying for her.
I suppose she felt too ashamed.
So there we were, not speaking.
Me because I was too angry,
Kim because she was too ashamed.
I knew we would have to speak soon.
There was something that had to be done.

6

Secrets

I'd already taken all the stolen clothes
out of Kim's wardrobe and put them
at the back of mine.
She must have known I'd taken them
but she still didn't say anything.

The first day that Mum went back to work
I waited for Kim to get back from school.
As soon as she walked through the door
I got the bag of clothes.
I dumped them at her feet.

She looked at me.

'When did you find them?' she asked.

'Ages ago,' I told her.

'Now you've got to get rid of them,
before anyone else finds them. Come on.'

I led her down to the common.
There was hardly anyone about,
just a couple of dog-walkers.
It was beginning to get cold and dark.
'Look,' I said, and pointed.
In the middle of the common was a huge bonfire.
It was all ready for the next day –
November 5th.

'I saw it the other day,' I said.
'I thought what a brilliant way to get rid of
the clothes. Burn them!'
I was so pleased with my idea
that I forgot I was supposed to be angry.
Kim even laughed,
for the first time since that Saturday.
She marched straight up to the bonfire.

There was a fence around it.
We waited until no one was around.
Then I helped Kim over.
She stuck the bag right into the middle
of the bonfire.
Behind old carpets and bits of wood.
'There,' she said, 'that should do.'

I helped her back over the fence
and she gave me a big hug.
I think she was trying to say thanks,
or sorry. Something like that.

The next night Kim came with Ian and me
to watch the fireworks.
We got there early
to watch them light the bonfire.
Little flames began to lick around the edge.
Then the whole lot went up.
We could feel the heat on our faces.
Kim and I smiled at each other.
A secret smile that Ian didn't notice.
Then Kim whispered in my ear, 'Thank you.'

So what can I tell you about my sister now?
Well, I think she's grown up a bit lately.
She's had a scare, and it's made her think.
She's got different friends now.
Friends that don't go looking for trouble.
Not that Kim's turned into a little angel –
but then I don't suppose she ever will.